Williamson **W** Publishing

Really Cool Felt Crafts

Peg Blanchette & Terri Thibault

Illustrations by
Marie Ferrante-Doyle

Quick Starts for Kids!™

WILLIAMSON PUBLISHING ◉ CHARLOTTE, VERMONT

Library of Congress Cataloging-in-Publication Data

Blanchette, Peg, 1949-
    Really cool felt crafts / Peg Blanchette & Terri Thibault ; illustrations by Marie Ferrante-Doyle.
        p. cm. -- (Quick starts for kids!)
    Includes index.
    ISBN 1-885593-80-5 (pbk.)
    1. Felt work. I. Title: Felt crafts. II. Thibault, Terri, 1954- III. Title. IV. Series.

TT880 .B547 2002
746'.0463--dc21

2002027010

Quick Starts for Kids!™ series editor: **Susan Williamson**
Interior design: **Sarah Rakitin**
Illustrations: **Marie Ferrante-Doyle**
Cover design: **Marie Ferrante-Doyle**
Cover photography: **Peter J. Coleman**
Printing: **Capital City Press**

Williamson Publishing Co.
P.O. Box 185
Charlotte, VT 05445
(800) 234-8791

Manufactured in the United States of America

10 9 8 7 6 5 4 3 2 1

Kids Can!®, *Little Hands*®, *Kaleidoscope Kids*®, and *Tales Alive!*® are registered trademarks of Williamson Publishing.

Good Times™, *Quick Starts for Kids!*™, *You Can Do It!*™, *Quick Starts Tips!*™, and *Quick Starts Jump-Starts*™ are trademarks of Williamson Publishing.

Dedication

To our children, who inspire us to imagine, to create, and to love, and who fill our lives with the anticipation of joys yet to come: Josh and Dan Blanchette, Tylor and Kazmin Thibault.

Acknowledgments

We would like to acknowledge and thank the "Road Nieces" for their assistance in testing our instructions and for giving us very helpful suggestions along the way: Jenni-Lu Delorge, Taylor, Ashley and Lindsey Thibault.

More *Quick Starts for Kids!*™ books by
Peg Blanchette & Terri Thibault
(See page 64 to order.)

Contents

Have Fun with Felt!

Several years ago, we began working (actually, we should say "playing") with felt. We made felt mitten ornaments — hundreds of them, and no two alike. Soon all of our friends and relatives had them, hanging on their Christmas trees, strung as garlands, and trimming their windows and doors. People saw us having so much fun making felt mittens that they started doing the same — we were even asked to come into teachers' classrooms to help the students make their own felt mitten ornaments to give as gifts! Since then, we've moved on to many other felt crafts, because we love working with this versatile fabric.

Felt is so easy to use (just cut and glue!), and its bright-colored possibilities are never-ending — from critters to clothing and everything between. It's pliable and forgiving, and just plain fun to work with. And, as we discovered, felt crafts are perfect for working on with a buddy — your imaginations *really* get going! We'll show you how to work with felt to make fun (and practical) projects to keep or to give as gifts. So call a friend or two, grab a few supplies, and CREATE!

Peg Blanchette
Terri Thibault

Quick Starts Tips!™

Make a craft box for extra-easy felting fun! In the mood to craft? Just pull out the boxes that contain what you've collected or need. Start with two boxes: one for collectibles, scraps, and trims and the other for craft scissors, fabric scissors, a glue gun and glue, tracing paper, pencils, and markers. Here's where you can put all those pieces of ribbon and yarn, felt scraps, plus shells, sea glass, glitter, pieces of old costume jewelry, beads, and buttons you have around, too. You can even decorate the boxes with felt and fun flower or frog designs — see pages 25 to 28 for details!

Felt Craft Supplies

The great thing about working with felt is that you hardly need any supplies — just the felt and some scissors and glue! Here are the basics to get you started:

Felt

You can buy felt in fabric or hobby/craft stores in precut 8¹/₂" x 11" (21 x 27.5 cm) or 12" x 18" (30 x 45 cm) "squares" (rectangles, actually!). Or you can buy felt by the yard from a *bolt* (that's just a fancy way of describing a big roll of fabric that's wrapped around a cardboard center). To trace patterns onto light- or medium-colored felt, we use a felt-tip marker. For dark felt, a piece of chalk works great. And best of all, you can trace onto either side of the felt, because both sides are exactly the same.

Scissors

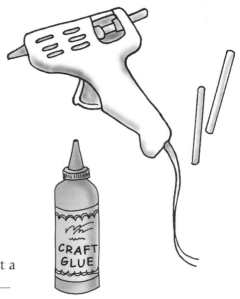

Fabric scissors are sharp scissors used to cut felt. Use them only for cutting fabric, felt, or cloth ribbons (not paper, or they'll get dull, real fast). For cutting paper or cardboard (to make your patterns, for instance) use regular *craft scissors*. *Pinking shears* are a special kind of fabric scissors with jagged edges, perfect for making decorative details.

Glue

We prefer to use a *glue gun* for felt projects because the hot glue makes the pieces stick together really well. *But, before using one, you need to get a grown-up's permission.* This small, inexpensive tool sometimes comes with "high" and "low" temperature settings, or you can buy individual "high temperature" or "low temperature" glue guns. Felt sticks together best with the "high temperature" setting or type. But be careful, the glue *is* hot, and it dries quickly, so just glue small areas at a time. If you don't have a glue gun on hand, use *craft glue,* which takes at least a few hours to dry. *Fabric glue* comes in bottles with pointed tips — great for drawing designs on felt. Then just sprinkle on the glitter!

Felt Hang-Ups

Part of the fun of crafting with felt is how one idea leads to another ... and another! Our String-a-Lings are a great example. What began as one simple felt animal gave inspiration to a whole corral of critters! Are you an animal lover? Hang your own personalized pet string-a-lings from your window, bedpost, closet door, bulletin board, or ceiling light fixture. Look around your bedroom for other ideas. Imagine your walls decorated with a bright Sunburst Banner ... or "crawling" with colorful Dragonfly Dangles — no two alike! Felt hang-ups look great anywhere!

Really Cool FELT CRAFTS

Dragonfly Dangles

What is it about dragonflies that we find so fascinating? Is it their iridescent coloring? Or the way they dance on the water? Whatever it is, we see them copied everywhere — in classrooms and stores, in bedrooms and kitchens, on clothing and beach towels. And with the bright colors of felt, you can make your own and hang them around your room or dangle them from your backpack.

Materials

+ *Template supplies:* tracing paper, craft scissors, cereal-box cardboard
+ Felt: two large pieces (at least 5 ¹/₂" x 8 ¹/₂" / 14 x 21 cm), blue (two wings and stripes) and orange (body); scraps of navy (antennae), black (eyes), and teal (a blue-green; for wing and body stripes)
+ Black felt-tip marker
+ Fabric scissors
+ Glue gun/glue
+ Ribbon or string, 8" (20 cm) piece

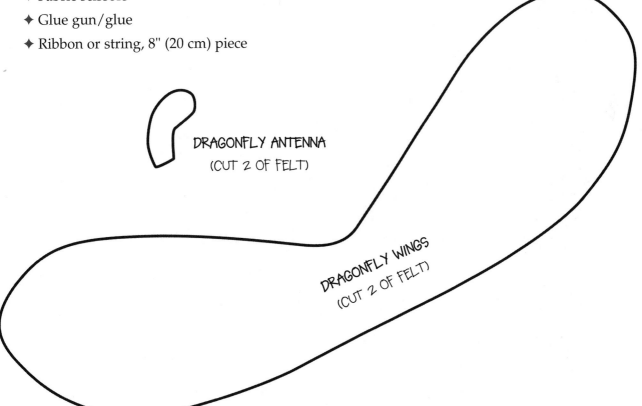

DRAGONFLY ANTENNA
(CUT 2 OF FELT)

DRAGONFLY WINGS
(CUT 2 OF FELT)

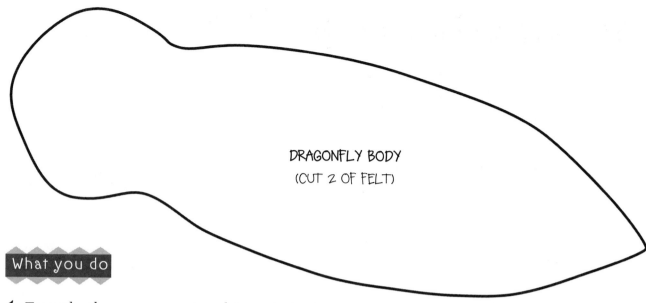

DRAGONFLY BODY
(CUT 2 OF FELT)

1. Trace the three DRAGONFLY templates onto tracing paper and cut out. Then, trace onto cardboard, label, and cut out.

2. Trace the cardboard patterns onto the different colors of felt using the marker. Cut out all the pieces.

3. Glue the wings to one body piece as shown. Fold the ribbon in half and glue to the top of head. Glue an antenna on each side of the ribbon. Then, glue the second body part on top.

4. Cut out and glue small black circles for the eyes. Using contrasting colors, cut thin strips of felt and glue them along the wings and down the back of the body. Trim any excess with scissors.

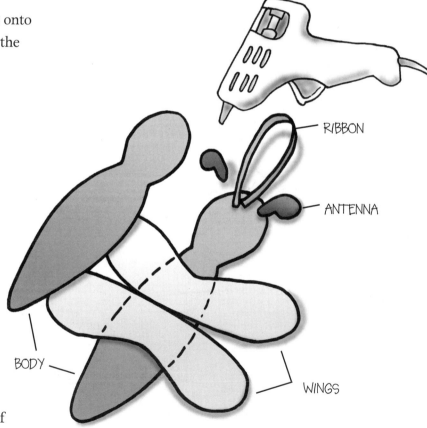

RIBBON

ANTENNA

BODY

WINGS

8

Sunburst Banner

The sun, the moon, and the stars — they never go out of style! Make your own big, bold, beautiful sunburst banner, personalized with your name, or a friend's. It's a grand sight to wake up to each morning!

Materials

✦ Felt: one 20" x 37" (50 x 94 cm) piece of a dark background color of your choice; three yellow precut 8 ½" x 11" (21 x 27.5 cm) sheets (sun); scraps (face details and lettering)

✦ Ruler

✦ Glue gun/glue

✦ Dowel or curtain rod, 25" long x 2" diameter (62.5 x 5 cm)

✦ *Template supplies:* tracing paper, craft scissors, cereal-box cardboard

✦ Black felt-tip marker/chalk

✦ Fabric scissors

✦ Silver sequin braid, about a yard (90 cm)

✦ Cording, bulky yarn, or string (to hang the banner)

✦ Pinking shears (optional)

✦ Tape

Quick Starts Tips!™

For the large felt background, you'll need to purchase felt from a bolt (page 5) in a fabric store. The sun and ray details and lettering can be cut from precut felt sheets or large scraps. Choose whatever colors you like. We used dark purple for the background and mouth, eye, and nose details, medium purple for the cheeks and eye centers, yellow for the sun, and gold for the lettering. But don't limit yourself — choose whatever colors *you* like best!

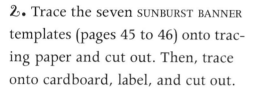
1. Fold down the top of the short side of the background felt. Glue the edge to the banner back, making a band for the dowel. This will be the back of your banner. Note: If you're using a thicker dowel, lay it on the banner, fold over enough felt to cover it, then glue the edge down and remove the dowel.

2. Trace the seven SUNBURST BANNER templates (pages 45 to 46) onto tracing paper and cut out. Then, trace onto cardboard, label, and cut out.

3. Trace the cardboard patterns onto the different colors of felt using the marker or chalk. For the sunburst, place the sun cardboard pattern against the fold. For the rays, you'll be able to fit six (two of each pattern) onto one precut sheet as shown. Cut out all the pieces.

4. Fold each ray in half lengthwise and cut two to three slits. Cut off a little bit from each side of the slit (this will allow the background felt to show through). Lay the sun's face and rays on the front of the banner, leaving room at the bottom for the name and fringe. Alternate the four sets of rays around the sun's face, leaving space between the face and rays for the sequin braid trim. Glue the face and rays in place.

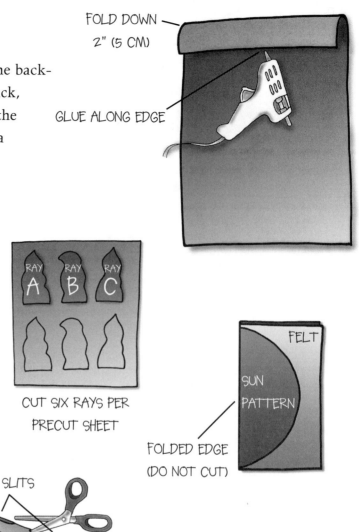

FOLD DOWN 2" (5 CM)

GLUE ALONG EDGE

CUT SIX RAYS PER PRECUT SHEET

FELT

SUN PATTERN

FOLDED EDGE (DO NOT CUT)

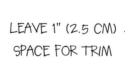

SLITS

CUT SLITS FOR RAYS

FOLD

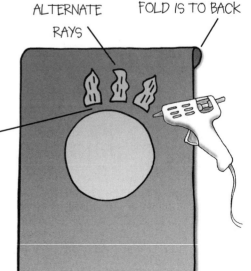

ALTERNATE RAYS

FOLD IS TO BACK

LEAVE 1" (2.5 CM) SPACE FOR TRIM

5. Cut a small slit in the center of the lips. Glue the lips, eyes, and eyebrows in place. To make the cheeks, cut circles and make pointy edges with scissors (or use pinking shears). Cut thin strips of felt to make the nose and eye lines; glue in place. Glue the sequin braid around the sun's face.

6. To make the fringe, tape across the banner, 4" (10 cm) up from the bottom edge. Cut strips along the bottom up to the tape; remove the tape. Cut out block letters and glue your name beneath the rays. Slide the dowel in place and tie on the cording to hang up your banner!

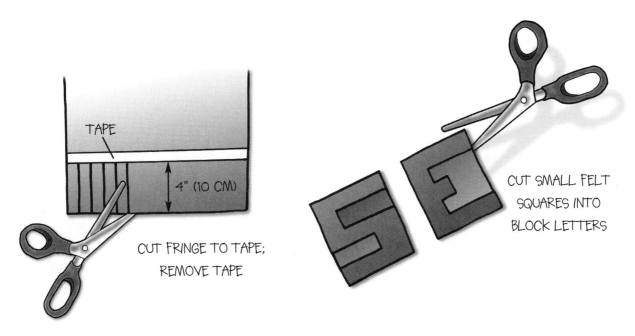

TAPE

4" (10 CM)

CUT FRINGE TO TAPE;
REMOVE TAPE

CUT SMALL FELT
SQUARES INTO
BLOCK LETTERS

Lindsey

More Quick Starts Fun!

Night and day. On the back side of your banner, make a man-in-the-moon shape (add stars, of course). Add a piece of decorative edging to cover where the banner is glued on the back. Now you've got a reversible banner!

String-a-Lings

OK, we admit it — this project took on a life of its own! What started out as a little bird on a string quickly turned into a whole family, and the bunny and dog followed. We just didn't know when to stop! You can do the same — don't feel limited to the animals here or even to the number of dangling accessories. Are you a dog person? Make several dogs in different colors and give them each their own personalized food dish and bone (or add a ball, doghouse, or hydrant!). Stretch your imagination as you string-a-ling!

Materials

- *Template supplies:* tracing paper, craft scissors, cereal-box cardboard
- Felt: 8 ½" x 11" (21 x 27.5 cm) precut sheets and scraps in the colors of your choice
- Black and pink felt-tip markers
- Fabric scissors
- Glue gun/glue
- Ribbon or string (in coordinating colors), about 30" (75 cm) for each string-a-ling (for hanging)
- Ruler
- Cotton batting or scraps (for stuffing)
- Hole punch
- Pinking shears
- Pom-poms, 4 small black ones (for dog and bunny eyes); 1 large white (for bunny's tail)
- Bells, 1 small for each string-a-ling (optional)

Note: As cute as these string-a-lings are, be sure they are not hung over a child's crib or within a toddler's reach. They have many removable parts that could cause choking.

Really Cool FELT CRAFTS

For each string-a-ling

1. Trace the STRING-A-LING templates (pages 46 to 48) onto tracing paper and cut out. Then, trace onto cardboard, label, and cut out.

2. Trace the cardboard patterns onto the felt using the black marker. Cut out all the pieces.

3. Glue the string or ribbon down the middle of one body piece, leaving about 8" (20 cm) above the head to make the hanging loop.

4. Cut out the additional detail pieces as noted in the illustrations. Assemble the body and details, leaving an opening at the body bottom or side for stuffing. Then glue closed, tie a bell to the bottom of the string (if you wish), tie a loop at the top, and hang up your string-a-ling!

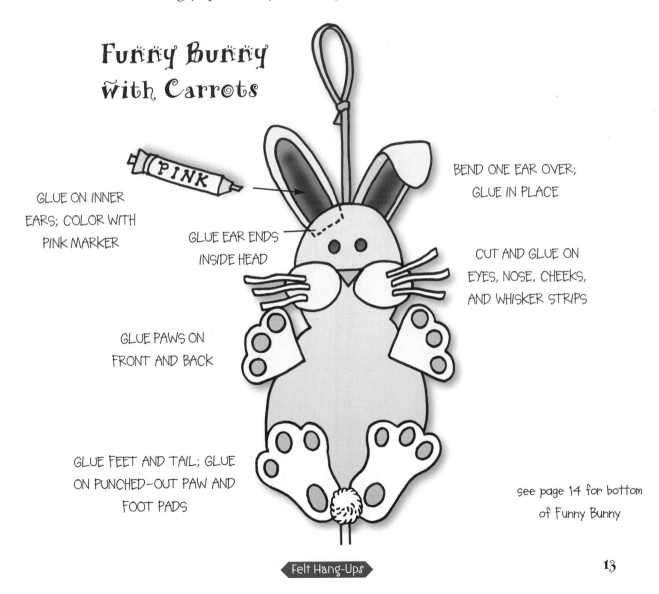

Funny Bunny with Carrots

GLUE ON INNER EARS; COLOR WITH PINK MARKER

PINK

GLUE EAR ENDS INSIDE HEAD

BEND ONE EAR OVER; GLUE IN PLACE

CUT AND GLUE ON EYES, NOSE, CHEEKS, AND WHISKER STRIPS

GLUE PAWS ON FRONT AND BACK

GLUE FEET AND TAIL; GLUE ON PUNCHED-OUT PAW AND FOOT PADS

see page 14 for bottom of Funny Bunny

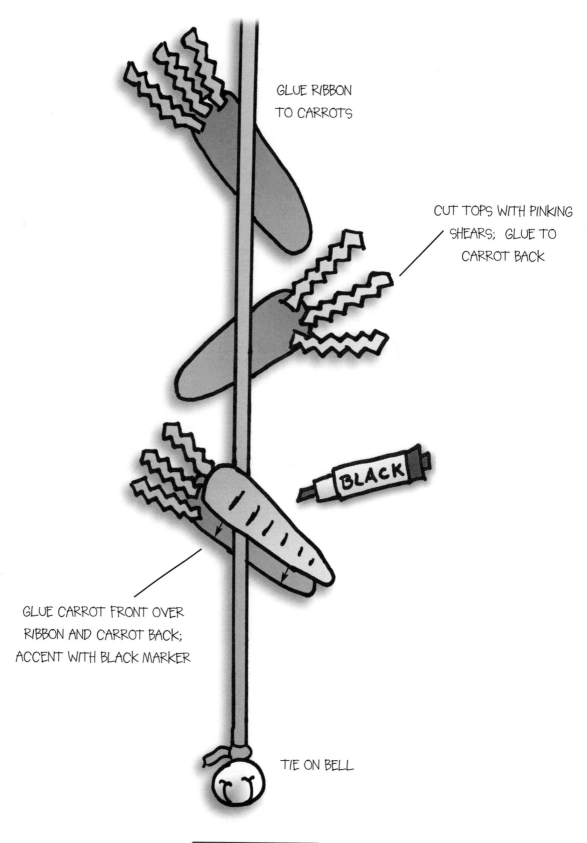

GLUE RIBBON
TO CARROTS

CUT TOPS WITH PINKING
SHEARS; GLUE TO
CARROT BACK

BLACK

GLUE CARROT FRONT OVER
RIBBON AND CARROT BACK;
ACCENT WITH BLACK MARKER

TIE ON BELL

Really Cool FELT CRAFTS

Fido on a String

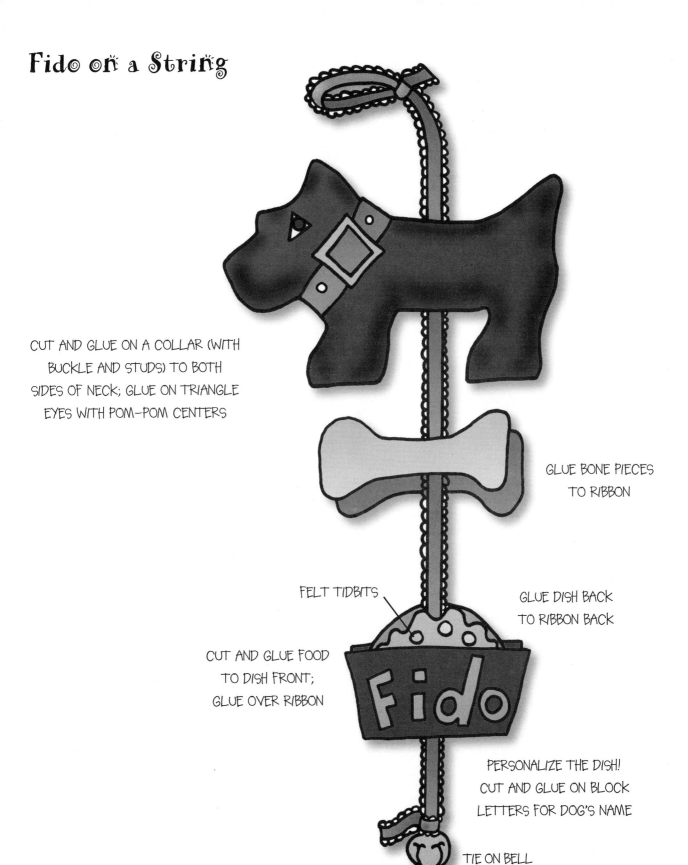

CUT AND GLUE ON A COLLAR (WITH BUCKLE AND STUDS) TO BOTH SIDES OF NECK; GLUE ON TRIANGLE EYES WITH POM-POM CENTERS

GLUE BONE PIECES TO RIBBON

FELT TIDBITS

GLUE DISH BACK TO RIBBON BACK

CUT AND GLUE FOOD TO DISH FRONT; GLUE OVER RIBBON

PERSONALIZE THE DISH! CUT AND GLUE ON BLOCK LETTERS FOR DOG'S NAME

TIE ON BELL

Nesting Birds

GLUE WING TO EACH SIDE;
CUT AND GLUE ON EYES

GLUE TAIL FEATHERS
TO BODY BACKS; CUT
AND GLUE ON BEAKS

CONTRASTING
TAIL FEATHERS

WING

GLUE ON BODY FRONTS,
STUFF, AND GLUE CLOSED

TAIL FEATHER

WING

CUT AND GLUE BEAK BETWEEN
EACH NESTING BIRD'S HEAD; GLUE
ON FELT OR POM-POM EYES

GLUE HEADS TO NEST
BACK; GLUE ON RIBBON
AND NEST FRONT

CUT AND GLUE ON
CONTRASTING STRIPS
FOR TWIGS

TIE ON BELL

Felt Favorites

The crafts included here are perfect for creating with felt, and — you guessed it — they're some of our favorites. Make a special bank shaped as a felt penguin (you lift its beak to deposit the money), a comfy pillow, Raggedy Ann and Andy dolls, a designed-by-you jewelry box or treasure chest, or super-original pencil toppers. Use our ideas for starters, then try your own. You may even discover a better design or method that works for you — great! After all, you're the artist, and these are your projects!

Quick Starts Tips!™

Scrap it. As you're crafting, keep the scraps — they're great for the finishing touches, and nothing is wasted.

Perky Penguin Bank

Are you saving up for something special? Let's face it, we all need an incentive to save money! Place your savings in the bank … a penguin bank, that is! This perky penguin will be very happy to collect your money as it sits on your bureau, bedside table, or desk. And only you will know what's inside, under the penguin's beak!

Materials

✦ *Template supplies:* tracing paper, craft scissors, tape, cereal-box cardboard
✦ Felt: two black precut 12" x 18" (30 x 45 cm) sheets; one white precut 8 ½" x 11" (21 x 27.5 cm) sheets; scraps of yellow (beak) and orange (feet)
✦ White chalk; black felt-tip marker
✦ Fabric scissors
✦ Ruler
✦ Glue gun/glue
✦ Bottle, approximately 9" (22.5 cm) high, with a 1 ½" (4 cm) opening (a juice bottle is fine, just be sure the opening is wide enough to accept quarters)

What you do

1. Trace the seven PERKY PENGUIN templates (pages 49 to 51) onto tracing paper and cut out. Tape the PENGUIN BODY TOP and BOTTOM tracing-paper templates together to make the full pattern. Trace all the patterns onto cardboard, label, and cut out.

2. Trace the full body, wing (twice), tail, and bow tie patterns onto the black felt using chalk. Trace the belly/face pattern onto the white felt, and the foot pattern (twice) onto the orange felt using the marker. Cut out all the pieces.

3. Glue the belly/face piece to one of the body pieces, leaving a ³/₄" (2 cm) space between the top edges.

Really Cool FELT CRAFTS

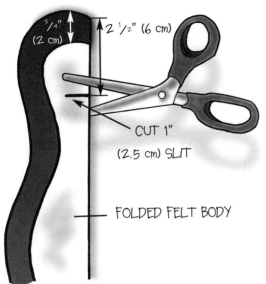

3/4" (2 cm)

2 1/2" (6 cm)

CUT 1" (2.5 cm) SLIT

FOLDED FELT BODY

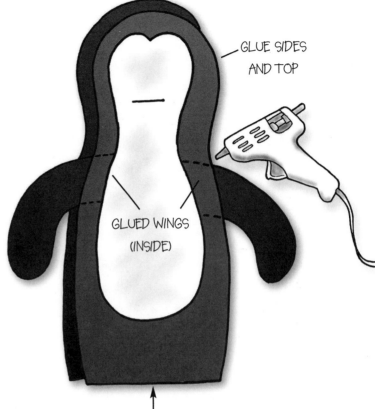

GLUE SIDES AND TOP

GLUED WINGS (INSIDE)

LEAVE BOTTOM OPEN

4. Fold these glued pieces in half lengthwise. Measure 2 ¹/₂" (6 cm) down from the top and cut a 1" (2.5 cm) slit for the opening under the beak. When you lay the piece flat, you'll have a 2" (5 cm) opening.

5. Glue the two wings on the top of the second body piece. Glue the two body pieces together along the outside edges, leaving the bottom open.

6. Glue feet to the body front; glue tail to body back. Cut out and glue a center on the bow tie; glue bow tie to the penguin's neck. Cut out a yellow beak shape; glue so it curves above the slit. Cut out black eyes and glue on.

7. Slip the penguin over the bottle and start dropping in your hard-earned coins! (See, saving money *is* fun!)

Pencil Toppers & Finger Puppets

We had so much fun making these that we didn't want to stop! Whether you make them for your fingertips, pockets, or pencil tops, they'll be a big hit. Let your imagination go for a ride — to the zoo, the circus, on a safari, even to a rodeo. Start with the ideas here or make your own cool collections. And be prepared to have lots of fun!

Materials

✦ *Template supplies:* tracing paper, craft scissors, cereal-box cardboard
✦ Felt scraps, in the colors of your choice
✦ Black felt-tip marker
✦ Fabric scissors
✦ Glue gun/glue
✦ Pom-poms, wiggle eyes, and assorted trims
✦ Pinking shears

What you do

For each pencil topper and finger puppet

1. Trace the PENCIL TOPPER or FINGER PUPPET templates (pages 51 to 54) onto tracing paper and cut out. Then, trace onto cardboard, label, and cut out.

2. Trace the cardboard patterns onto the felt using the marker. Cut out the felt pieces.

3. Glue the head/body pieces together along the top and side edges, leaving the bottom edge open (very important!).

Note: The *horse, rabbit,* and *elephant* need to have parts glued to one side of the head *before* gluing the second head piece on top. See specific illustrations.

4. Add felt details and other decorations as noted.

Really Cool FELT CRAFTS

Horse

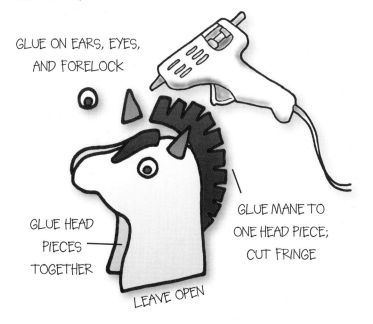

GLUE ON EARS, EYES,
AND FORELOCK

GLUE HEAD
PIECES
TOGETHER

GLUE MANE TO
ONE HEAD PIECE;
CUT FRINGE

LEAVE OPEN

Quick Starts Tips!™

◎ **We used wiggle eyes** for
our toppers/puppets, but you
could also use small black
pom-poms or cut out small
pieces from felt scraps.

◎ **To make any of them two-
sided,** just repeat the details
on both sides!

More Quick Starts Fun!

Pocket people. Follow the directions as if you were
going to make finger puppets, but stuff cotton balls
or batting in the opening and glue it shut. Attach ribbon or string and tie pocket people to your backpack,
belt loops, and barrettes ... or put in your pockets!

Felt Favorites

Rabbit

GLUE EARS TO ONE HEAD PIECE

GLUE HEADS TOGETHER

LEAVE OPEN

GLUE ON EYES, FELT CHEEK CIRCLES, POM-POM NOSE, AND GRAY FELT WHISKERS; USE MARKERS TO SHADE EARS AND TO DRAW TEETH

Penguin

GLUE BELLY ON

LEAVE OPEN

GLUE BODIES TOGETHER

FOLD BEAK IN HALF; GLUE BOTTOM HALF ONTO FACE

FOLD

GLUE WINGS TO SHOULDERS

GLUE ON BOW TIE, EYES, AND FEET

Alligator ... SNAP!

TEETH

GLUE FELT JAW (WITH TEETH ALREADY IN PLACE)

GLUE HEADS TOGETHER

LEAVE OPEN

GLUE ON EYES

CUT WITH PINKING SHEARS ALONG THIS EDGE

22

Elephant

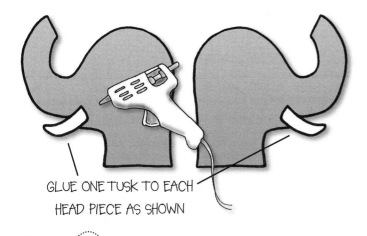

GLUE ONE TUSK TO EACH HEAD PIECE AS SHOWN

GLUE HEADS TOGETHER (WITH TUSKS INSIDE)

GLUE ON EYES

AND EARS

LEAVE OPEN

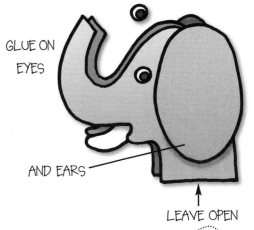

Dog

USE MARKER TO DRAW MOUTH

GLUE HEADS TOGETHER

LEAVE OPEN

GLUE ON FELT NOSE AND EARS; GLUE ON EYES

FOR KERCHIEF, CUT AND GLUE ON TWO FELT TRIANGLES

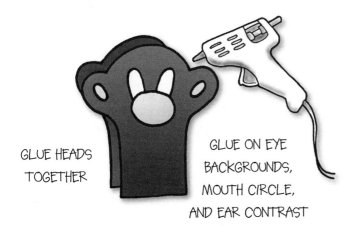

Monkey

GLUE HEADS TOGETHER

GLUE ON EYE BACKGROUNDS, MOUTH CIRCLE, AND EAR CONTRAST

GLUE ON A FELT HAT, WITH POM-POM AND HATBAND

GLUE ON EYES, FELT NOSE AND BOW TIE; DRAW ON SMILE WITH MARKER

LEAVE OPEN

Frog

GLUE ON EYE
BACKGROUNDS

GLUE BODIES
TOGETHER

GLUE ON EYES, CHEEK
SPOTS, AND TONGUE

LEAVE OPEN
BETWEEN MARKS

Clown

GLUE HEADS
TOGETHER

GLUE ON FELT
CHEEKS, NOSE, SMILE,
HAIR, AND EYES

GLUE ON COLLAR,
THEN BOW TIE

PINKING
SHEARS GIVE
HAIR A FANCY EDGE

LEAVE OPEN

Party Hat

GLUE HATS
TOGETHER

GLUE ON
POM-POM AND
PUNCHED-OUT
DESIGNS

FRINGE ONE SIDE OF
HATBAND BEFORE
GLUING IN PLACE

LEAVE OPEN
BETWEEN MARKS

Really Cool FELT CRAFTS

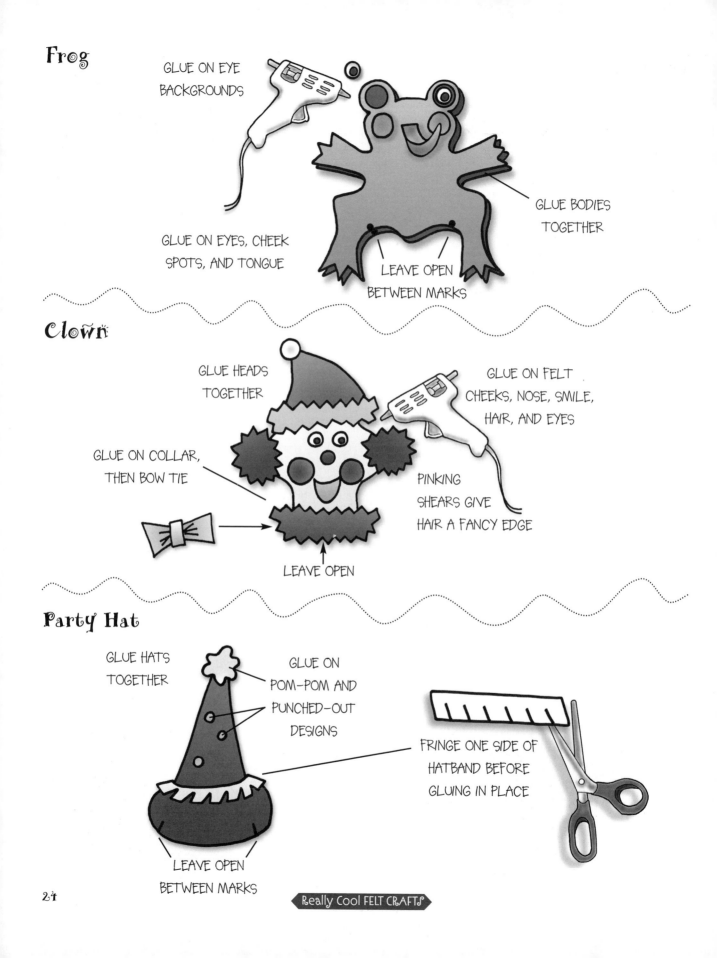

Terrific Treasure Chests

Collections of marbles, shells, rocks, coins, barrettes, scrunchies — they're in your room, but where? Probably all over the place! By reusing a box, you can create your very own treasure chest to store them. (We used an old greeting-card box, but the size of your treasure chest is entirely up to you!) You could even decorate boxes of different sizes for each of your collections. Start with the frog or flower design shown here, and then make up your own. Just imagine three or four brightly colored containers on your bureau that are fun to look at … and help keep your treasures safe, too!

Materials

✦ Box, about 2" x 6 ½" x 8 ½" (5 x 16 x 21 cm), or any size you want
✦ Felt: four pieces, one large enough to cover the top and sides of the box, the other large enough for the bottom and sides, and one or two rectangles to cover the back of the chest; scraps for frog and flower, in the colors of your choice
✦ Glue gun/glue
✦ Fabric scissors
✦ Duct tape
✦ Ribbon or lace, for decorative edging

Additional Frog and Flower decorations:

✦ *Template supplies:* tracing paper, craft scissors, cereal-box cardboard
✦ Felt scraps of assorted colors
✦ Black felt-tip marker
✦ Pom-poms: 1 medium (flower), 2 small (frog eyes), 1 tiny (tongue bug)
✦ Cotton balls, batting, or felt scraps (to stuff frog)

What you do

First, cover the box …

1. Center the box top, upside down, on one of the large felt pieces.

2. Glue the felt to the top, then glue to the front and sides. (Leave the back of the box unglued for now.) You'll have extra felt at the front corners. Just dab some glue inside each flap and pinch together. Then, fold to the side, and glue in place. Trim off any excess felt along the top edges.

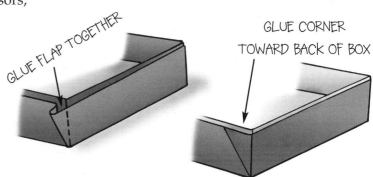

GLUE FLAP TOGETHER

GLUE CORNER TOWARD BACK OF BOX

3. Repeat steps 1 and 2 for the box bottom.

4. Place the box top over the bottom, so they meet but don't overlap. Put duct tape over the back seam, inside and out, for the "hinge." Glue the felt to the back top and bottom. Fold and glue the corners to the back.

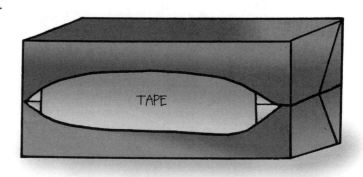

5. Glue on the rectangle of felt (or two pieces, if you prefer) to cover the back.

6. Glue decorative ribbon or lace trim along the top sides.

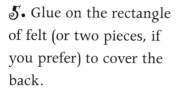

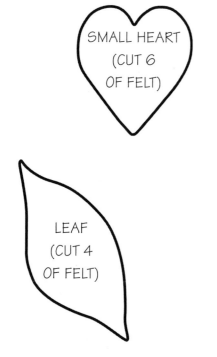

SMALL HEART
(CUT 6
OF FELT)

LEAF
(CUT 4
OF FELT)

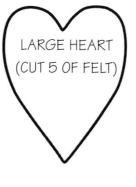

LARGE HEART
(CUT 5 OF FELT)

... then decorate!

Flower Power!

1. Trace the HEART and LEAF templates onto tracing paper; cut out. Then, trace onto cardboard, label, and cut out.

2. Trace the cardboard patterns onto different colors of felt using the marker. You'll need five large hearts, three small hearts, and two leaves for the flower. You'll need three small hearts for the bud. For contrast, use two different heart colors (petals and buds) and two shades of green for the leaves. Cut out all the pieces.

Really Cool FELT CRAFTS

3. Glue the five large heart shapes in a circle in the center of the box top. Glue three of the smaller heart shapes on top of the larger heart circle. Glue on a colorful pom-pom for the center.

4. Form the leaf by pinching the bottom and adding a dab of glue to hold the sides together. There you have it … instant leaf! Place the two leaves around the side edges of the flower.

5. Using the three small heart shapes left, roll one heart as the bud center. Fold and glue the next heart around the first one; fold and glue the third heart around the other two on the opposite side. Cut a small rectangle of green felt to use as the bud "vase" and glue around the bottom.

6. Decide where you want the flower bud to be and glue in place, attaching the two remaining leaves on either side. Having fun making the flower buds? Make some more and position them all over the box top or arrange them in a bunch. It's your treasure chest … go for it!

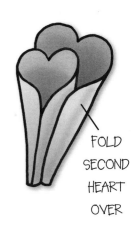

PINCH ONE END
TOGETHER AND GLUE ➝

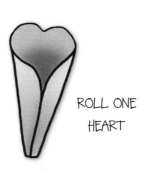

ROLL ONE
HEART

FOLD
SECOND
HEART
OVER

FOLD THIRD HEART
ON OPPOSITE SIDE

Picture this! Use your treasure chest to store your favorite pictures. Cut out more of the large hearts and glue them on top so there's a space in the middle for a picture.

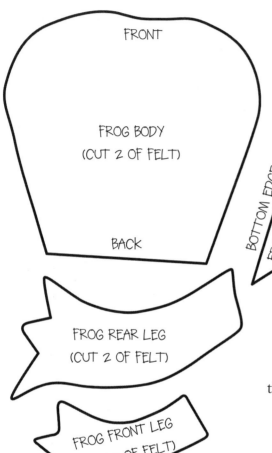

FRONT

FROG BODY
(CUT 2 OF FELT)

BACK

BOTTOM EDGE
FROG EYE SOCKET
(CUT 2 OF FELT)

FROG REAR LEG
(CUT 2 OF FELT)

FROG FRONT LEG
(CUT 2 OF FELT)

Frog in a Bog

1. Trace the FROG templates onto tracing paper and cut out. Then, trace onto cardboard, label, and cut out.

2. Trace the cardboard patterns onto felt using the marker. For contrast, use a different shade of green for the legs and eye sockets. Cut out all the pieces.

3. Glue the two frog body pieces together around the edges, leaving an opening at the mouth. Stuff the frog's body cavity.

4. Cut out a tongue and glue it below the frog's mouth. Glue the mouth opening together, then glue the frog's legs in place.

5. Glue the frog to the box top. To add the eyes, glue the sides of the eye sockets together, glue a pom-pom inside, and glue to the frog's head.

6. Finish by gluing a tiny black pom-pom "bug" on the tip of the frog's tongue and some spots to its back!

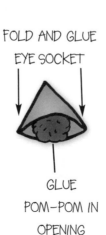

FOLD AND GLUE
EYE SOCKET

GLUE
POM-POM IN
OPENING

GLUE ON LEGS, TONGUE,
AND OTHER DETAILS

Wizard Pillow

People have been fascinated by wizards and magic potions as long as amazing tales have been told. We've always loved the tales of King Arthur and Merlin. Today, Harry Potter and Hagrid have captured the hearts of people everywhere. Even though you can't turn a toad into a prince (or can you?), you can still create a magical mood by making this Wizard Pillow. We guarantee you'll hear a lot of oohs and aahs when your friends see this pillow on your bed!

Quick Starts Tips!™

For the large felt pieces, you'll need to purchase felt from a bolt (page 5). The "details" can be cut from smaller precut felt sheets. Choose whatever colors you like. We used teal (a kind of blue-green) for the background and scraps of purple (hatband), white (beard and mustache), beige (face), yellow (star), and black (hat and eye).

Materials

- *Template supplies:* tracing paper, craft scissors, tape, cereal-box cardboard
- Felt: two 18 ¹/₂" x 18 ¹/₂" (46 x 46 cm) pieces of your background color; sheets or scraps in the colors of your choice (hat, hatband, face, beard, mustache, and star)
- Black felt-tip marker
- Fabric scissors
- Glue gun/glue
- Pillow form or insert, 16" (40 cm) square (available at craft stores)
- Fabric glue
- Glitter
- Plastic stars (or make them from felt scraps) and sequins, for the hat

What you do

1. Trace the seven WIZARD templates (pages 54 to 56) onto tracing paper and cut them out. Tape the BEARD TOP and BOTTOM tracing-paper templates together to make the full pattern. Then, trace all the patterns onto cardboard, label, and cut out.

2. Trace the cardboard patterns onto the different colors of felt using the marker. Cut out all the pieces.

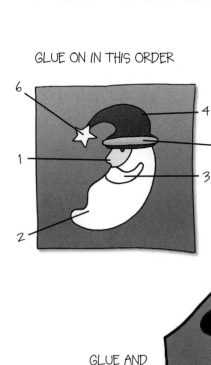

GLUE ON IN THIS ORDER

3. Using the glue gun or craft glue, glue the pieces onto one piece of the background felt in this order: face, beard, mustache, hat, hatband, star.

4. Place the pillow form between the two pieces of background felt, with the design on top. To glue around the felt edges, glue a small area and press the two sides together. Then, glue the next small area, and press together. *Hint:* Doing this step in stages will help you keep the side edges even, as you make your way around the pillow.

GLUE AND PRESS

5. Using the fabric glue, "draw" lines of glue along the beard and mustache, as well as outside the star. Sprinkle the glitter on the glue and let dry. (It will take a few hours to completely dry, so don't rush. Leaving it overnight is a good rule.) When the glue is completely dry, shake off any excess glitter.

6. Glue sequins, stars, or other decorations to the hat.

More Quick Starts Fun!

Overnight delight! Make a matching Wizard Pillow into a P.J. Tote (perfect for sleepovers). Leave the top edge of the pillow open and attach a shoulder strap: Just fold a 4" x 30" (10 x 75 cm) strip of matching felt in half and glue it together, so that you have a sturdy strap that's 2" (5 cm) wide. Attach it to the tote by gluing or, for a stronger hold, stitch it in place by hand. Then toss in your pj's, a toothbrush, your favorite stuffed animal — and have fun!

Really Cool FELT CRAFTS

The Raggedies

We've both had a Raggedy Ann or Andy doll at one time or another — but not back to back … until now! *Their smiling faces will bring a smile right back to your face!*

Materials

+ *Template supplies:* tracing paper, craft scissors, cereal-box cardboard
+ Felt: one white precut 8 $^1/_2$" x 11" (21 x 27.5 cm) sheet; scraps of red, black, blue, purple, pink (clothing and other details)
+ Black felt-tip marker
+ Fabric scissors
+ Glue gun/glue
+ Hole punch or small pom-poms (4 black for eyes and 4 red for noses and buttons)
+ Pinking shears
+ Thin ribbon, two 6" (15 cm) pieces (for hair ties)
+ Button or sequins (for Raggedy Ann's collar)

What you do

1. Trace the six RAGGEDY templates (pages 56 to 57) onto tracing paper and cut out. Then, trace onto cardboard, label, and cut out.

2. Trace the cardboard patterns onto the felt using the marker. You'll need two of the body pieces and suspenders; one dress, pair of shorts, and collar; and four shoes. Cut out all the pieces, making two of the shoes slightly wider than the pattern. For the body, fold the white felt sheet in half and trace and cut the two pieces at one time. Glue the two bodies together.

3. Glue the face pieces as shown, with pom-poms or punched-out circles of black felt for the eyes; a pom-pom or red felt circles for the noses; red strips for the mouths, and pink felt circles for the cheeks.

Use pinking shears to cut strips of red felt in varying lengths for hair. Bad hair day? Great! We like to make the hair on Andy's head really stick out! For Raggedy Ann, use longer pieces, and don't forget to give her bangs! Make a "braid" by gathering a few strands of hair on each side of her face and tying it with ribbon.

4. Now for clothes! Dress Raggedy Ann in a blue dress with red trim (use pinking shears to give it a zigzag edge), and add two pockets cut from scraps. Glue on the collar piece and a decorative button. Andy wears blue shorts and suspenders (with red pom-poms or felt for buttons). Add a purple bow tie and one red pocket cut from scraps.

5. Cut and glue on thin strips of red felt for striped tights; trim the strips after you've glued them in place. Glue shoes to each Raggedy, adding a black strap for Ann's.

USE PINKING SHEARS FOR HAIR

TRIM STRIPS AFTER GLUING

ADD A BLACK STRAP TO RAGGEDY ANN'S SHOES

More Quick Starts Fun!

Round Raggedies. Make a stuffed Raggedy Ann or Raggedy Andy doll! Before gluing the body pieces together, leave an opening and stuff it with cotton batting. Glue shut.

Fun Felt Wearables

Felt is easy to work with … and great to wear, too! It is washable, comes in a variety of colors, and can be purchased by the yard, so there's no end to the possibilities for your wardrobe and accessories. In just an hour, you can make a hat that's warm, soft, and comfy. Or, how about a felt pouch to carry or for storing doll clothes or hair stuff? Need a disguise? Craft a fun felt mask of your own design. When you've finished your own felt wardrobe, start on a smaller set. With felt, you can make one-of-a-kind doll or stuffed animal outfits at a fraction of the cost of store-bought. And it's a lot more fun to craft them yourself, in the style you like best!

Butterfly Mask

Turn yourself into a beautiful butterfly! Or, turn the template upside down and create something totally different. Use reddish-brown felt, add feathers and sequins, and you're a foxy fox. Whether you wear these masks or hang them from your bedpost or bulletin board, you'll have a blast!

Materials

+ *Template supplies:* tracing paper, craft scissors, cereal-box cardboard
+ Felt: one bright yellow precut 8 $^1/_2$" x 11" (21 x 27.5 cm) sheet, plus scraps in the colors of your choice
+ Black felt-tip marker
+ Fabric scissors
+ Glue gun/glue
+ Green craft feathers, 2 (antennae)
+ Pinking shears
+ Hole punch
+ Elastic string, about 12" (30 cm)

What you do

1. Trace the three BUTTERFLY templates (pages 58 to 59) onto tracing paper and cut out. Then, trace onto cardboard, and cut out. Trace and cut out the eyes, too!

Quick Starts Tips!™

More masks. You'll use the cardboard butterfly to make the actual mask. If you want to make more masks, make an extra cardboard butterfly pattern and label it, along with the body and wing cardboard patterns, for later tracings.

2. Lay the cardboard mask on the yellow felt; trace with the marker, and cut out. Glue the felt mask onto the cardboard mask.

3. Trace and cut the felt butterfly body and glue it to the mask; add details.

4. Cut out and glue on felt accent pieces. To make the swirls, cut a spiral design in two felt circles; glue in place. Cut, flare, and glue the wings (we used pinking shears to get a jagged effect on the wing decorations). Punch holes at the outer edge, and tie the elastic string to hold your mask on.

BODY

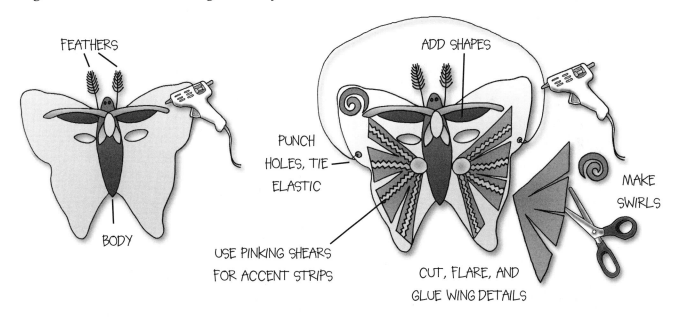

FEATHERS

BODY

ADD SHAPES

PUNCH HOLES, TIE ELASTIC

USE PINKING SHEARS FOR ACCENT STRIPS

CUT, FLARE, AND GLUE WING DETAILS

MAKE SWIRLS

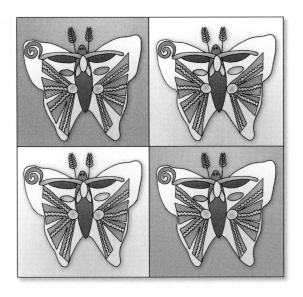

More Quick Starts Fun!

Hang it up! Turn your mask into a wall hanging. Instead of gluing the felt onto cardboard, glue it to a larger square (about 9"/22.5 cm) of solid-colored felt. Use four bright background colors with contrasting accent colors to make four butterfly "pictures." Glue or sew the squares together and hang it from a dowel rod (see page 10). Now that's art!

Rolled-Brim Hat

What's new in fashion these days? Hats — again! This rolled-brim hat is a snap to make. If you intend to wear your hat a lot, we suggest you sew it together, rather than gluing.

Materials

✦ *Template supplies:* tracing paper, craft scissors, tape, cereal-box cardboard
✦ Ruler
✦ Felt: two 12" x 18" (30 x 45 cm) pieces in the color of your choice; two 2" x 12" (5 x 30 cm) pieces in a contrasting color for the hatband
✦ Black felt-tip marker
✦ Fabric scissors
✦ Straight pins
✦ Glue gun/glue
✦ Needle and thread (optional)
✦ Pinking shears
✦ Buttons or other finishing touches

What you do

1. Trace the ROLLED-BRIM HAT template (page 59) onto tracing paper and cut it out. Cut a 6" (15 cm) square of tracing paper and tape it to the tracing-paper template. Trace the entire half-hat template onto cardboard. Label and cut out.

2. Fold one large felt piece in half the long way. Place the cardboard pattern against the fold and trace using the marker. Cut along the line. Repeat for the other felt piece.

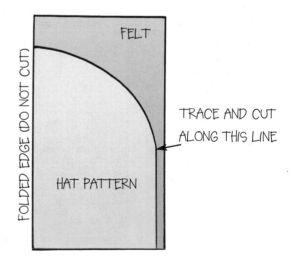

FELT

FOLDED EDGE (DO NOT CUT)

TRACE AND CUT ALONG THIS LINE

HAT PATTERN

Really Cool FELT CRAFTS

3. On one of the hat pieces, mark about 6" (15 cm) up from the bottom edge on each side. Pin the two hat pieces together, matching edges evenly, then glue or sew (see THE RUNNING STITCH, page 38) around the top, from mark to mark, about ¹/₄" (5 mm) in from the edge (this is the *seam allowance*). With scissors, clip in about 1/4" (5 mm) where you made the mark. Now turn the hat right side out.

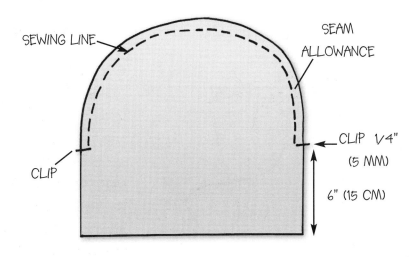

SEWING LINE

SEAM ALLOWANCE

CLIP ¹/4" (5 MM)

6" (15 CM)

CLIP

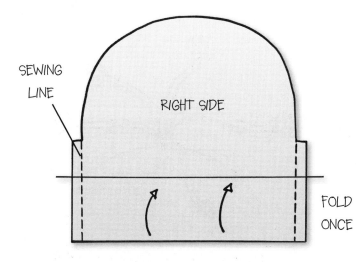

SEWING LINE

RIGHT SIDE

FOLD ONCE

4. Glue or sew the lower 6" (15 cm) of the hat sides together. Roll the brim up 2" (5 cm), then another 2" (5 cm).

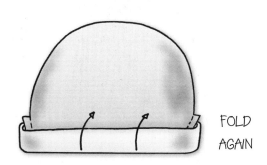

FOLD AGAIN

5. Hold the brim in place with a few stitches to keep it from unrolling. To make a decorative band, cut with pinking shears along the outer edges of the remaining felt piece. Glue the bands to the hat, beginning and ending at a side seam. Trim away any excess felt. Add buttons. Don't like buttons? Use beads, pearls, cutout felt shapes — you're the designer!

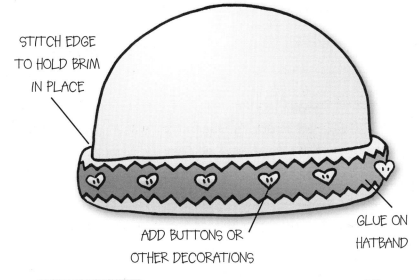

STITCH EDGE TO HOLD BRIM IN PLACE

ADD BUTTONS OR OTHER DECORATIONS

GLUE ON HATBAND

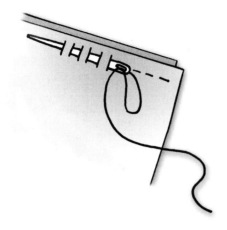

The Running Stitch

We recommend you use a running stitch to sew your hat by hand. These short, even stitches will keep your hat from pulling apart at the seam, and since you make several stitches at a time, the sewing goes quickly.

To make a running stitch, thread the needle and knot the thread. Bring the needle through the felt. Work the tip of the needle in and out of the felt pieces to create three or four stitches, then pull the needle and thread through all the stitches. Continue this way until you finish the seam.

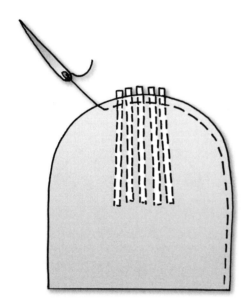

More Quick Starts Fun!

○ **Make it funny.** When you sew the hat seam (step 3), insert five ribbons (each about 7"/17.5 cm long and in different colors) into the top center. Pull the ribbons down between the two layers of felt so only about 1" (2.5 cm) is showing. Continue sewing, making sure to sew through the ribbons. Then, turn the hat right side out and tie bells on the ribbon ends. Fabulous!

○ **Have a hat party!** Invite all your stylish friends over to make their very own hats in bright colors, then take a group photo. This is a real memory-maker!

Doll Clothes Deluxe

When it comes to felt wearables, we think down a size or two, too — to our dolls! Take it from us: You're never too old to play with dolls or teddy bears, even if it just means dressing them in different outfits throughout the year. We have dolls in our homes that sit by the fire, dressed in their holiday best, which changes for the season and the special day, whether it's Hanukkah or Christmas, Valentine's Day, St. Patrick's Day, Passover or Easter, Mother's Day, July 4th, or Halloween! And doll clothes make great gifts for friends and family (especially for younger sisters!).

Using felt to make doll (or bear or bunny) clothes opens up a whole world of possibilities — and colors. The outfits here are just a guideline for what you can do. Have fun and be creative with the hat, vest, and skirt, as well as the tie-on sandals on page 42, decorating them to suit your tastes!

Materials

- *Template supplies:* tracing paper, craft scissors, cereal-box cardboard
- Felt: four precut 8 ½" x 11" (21 x 27.5 cm) sheets, two for the vest, two for the skirt, one for the hat; half a piece for the sandals; scraps for flower decorations, in the colors of your choice
- Black felt-tip marker
- Fabric scissors
- Glue gun/glue
- Small yellow and green pom-poms (flower centers)
- Narrow ribbon (for vest and sandals)
- Velcro circles (for skirt)
- Decorative flower (for hat)

What you do

For all doll clothes

1. Trace the 10 DOLL templates (pages 60 to 62) onto tracing paper and cut out. Then, trace all the patterns onto cardboard, label, and cut out.

2. Trace the cardboard patterns onto the felt using the marker. Cut out all the pieces.

Versatile Vest

1. Fold both felt pieces for the vest in half the short way. Place the vest back cardboard pattern on the fold of one piece, and the vest front pattern on the second piece as shown. Trace using the marker and cut out the three pieces.

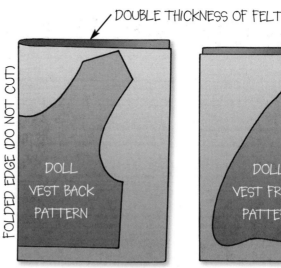

DOUBLE THICKNESS OF FELT

FOLDED EDGE (DO NOT CUT)

DOLL VEST BACK PATTERN

DOLL VEST FRONT PATTERN

FOLDED EDGE

2. Lay the vest back piece on your work surface and place the two front pieces on top. Glue at the sides, matching felt edges carefully. Turn the felt so the glued seam is on the inside, and try the vest on your doll (or bear), bringing the back shoulder flaps down over the front to fit. Glue the flaps in place.

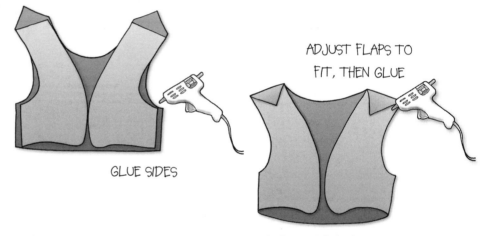

GLUE SIDES

ADJUST FLAPS TO FIT, THEN GLUE

TURN RIGHT SIDE OUT

3. To finish, tie two small bows with the ribbon and glue them on each shoulder flap.

From scraps of felt, trace and cut out flower petals, leaf, and stem; glue on vest front. Add a pom-pom to the flower center.

40

Simple Flowered Skirt

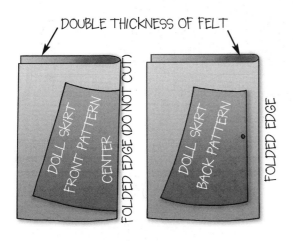

DOUBLE THICKNESS OF FELT

DOLL SKIRT FRONT PATTERN

CENTER

FOLDED EDGE (DO NOT CUT)

DOLL SKIRT BACK PATTERN

FOLDED EDGE

1. Fold both felt pieces for the skirt in half the short way. Place the skirt front cardboard pattern on the fold of one piece, and the skirt back pattern on the second piece as shown. Trace using the marker and cut out the three pieces.

2. Glue the two back pieces together, stopping halfway up from the bottom edge at the marked dot. Now glue the skirt back to the skirt front at each side, matching felt edges carefully. The back seam should be facing out (facing you) as you glue.

Glue backs together ...

LEAVE OPEN

SKIRT BACK

BACK

SIDE

GLUE TO DOT

... then glue back to front

GLUE SIDES

BACK SEAM

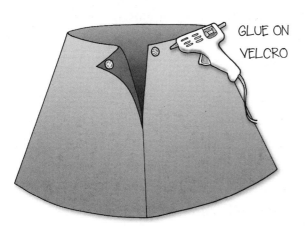

GLUE ON VELCRO

3. Turn skirt so glued seams are inside. Glue one side of the Velcro circle to the skirt back opening. Adjust the skirt to fit your doll's waist; then glue on the other Velcro circle. Add flowers on front to match the vest.

Snappy Hat

1. Fold the felt piece for the hat in half the short way. Trace the hat cardboard pattern *twice* onto the felt, placing the pattern on the fold each time (the pattern is only a fourth of the hat). Cut out. Glue the hat pieces together along the sides and top, leaving the bottom edge open.

2. With the glued seam facing you, fold the front brim up and glue in front. Glue the flower (or another decoration) to the center of the brim.

GLUE SIDES
AND TOP

LEAVE OPEN

FOLD UP BRIM AND
GLUE TO HOLD

GLUE ON
FLOWER

GLUE

PINCH TOGETHER
UNTIL DRY

Glue ribbon to bottom along outside edge

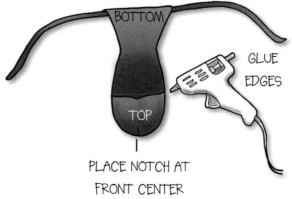

BOTTOM

TOP

GLUE
EDGES

PLACE NOTCH AT
FRONT CENTER

Easy-Tie Sandals

1. Trace the sandal bottom and the sandal top cardboard patterns *twice each* onto the half piece of felt and cut out.

2. Fold the sandal top in half lengthwise. Glue the notch and pinch it closed. When the glue is dry, turn so the right side is on top. Repeat for the other sandal top.

3. Place the top over the front of the sandal bottom. Glue around the edges. Repeat for the other sandal. Cut ribbon into two 15" (37.5 cm) pieces. Glue each ribbon to the outside back edge of each sandal. To wear, slip toes into top and tie ribbon around the doll's ankles.

Patriotic Pouch

Have you made that felt doll outfit (pages 39 to 42) yet? If so, you'll need a place to store the new clothes — and we've got just the thing. Or you can use it as a handy carry-along. The bag takes only a few minutes to put together, but the real fun is in the decorating — we did ours in red, white, and blue. Show off your patriotism, or pick other colors for your own look!

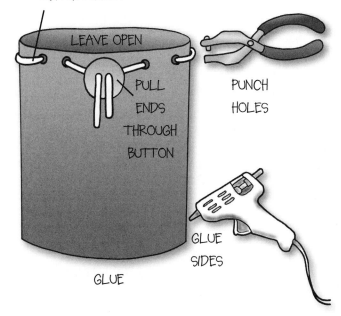

WEAVE RIBBON

LEAVE OPEN

PULL ENDS THROUGH BUTTON

PUNCH HOLES

GLUE SIDES

GLUE

Materials

- ✦ Fabric scissors
- ✦ Felt: two red precut 8 ½" x 11" (21 x 27.5 cm) sheets (we trimmed ours to measure 8 ½" x 9 ½"/21 x 24 cm — change the size if you wish); scraps of white and blue
- ✦ Glue gun/glue
- ✦ Hole punch
- ✦ Blue or white ribbon, 20" (50 cm)
- ✦ Large red button with large holes or four pom-poms
- ✦ *Template supplies:* tracing paper, craft scissors, cereal-box cardboard
- ✦ Ruler
- ✦ Black felt-tip marker

What you do

1. Trim the large felt pieces to the desired size. Glue together along the sides and bottom, matching edges evenly; leave the top open. For best results, glue a little at a time and press the felt edges together; then, move to the next spot and glue and press (page 30).

Punch holes along the top edge. Weave the ribbon through the holes so that the two ribbon ends come out the same hole on the front center (or along one of the sides, if you prefer). Thread each ribbon end through the button's holes and pull taut. Or, glue each ribbon end between two pom-poms and tie to close.

2. Trace the STAR template onto tracing paper and cut out. Then, trace onto cardboard, label, and cut out. Trace the cardboard pattern onto the white felt three times using the marker. Cut out all the pieces.

3. Cut 4" (10 cm) long strips of blue felt. Twist each strip two to three times, then glue each end onto the pouch front, along with the stars.

STAR
(CUT 3 — OR MORE! — OF FELT)

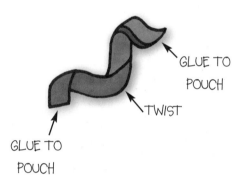

GLUE TO POUCH

TWIST

GLUE TO POUCH

More Quick Starts Fun!

Why wrap it when you can bag it? That's right, use this pouch as the wrapping for your next gift. Make one for your best friend's birthday (in his or her favorite colors); give one to your favorite Valentine (in red and white, covered with pink and red hearts); wrap your parents' Christmas gift (in red and green with little white mittens).

Templates

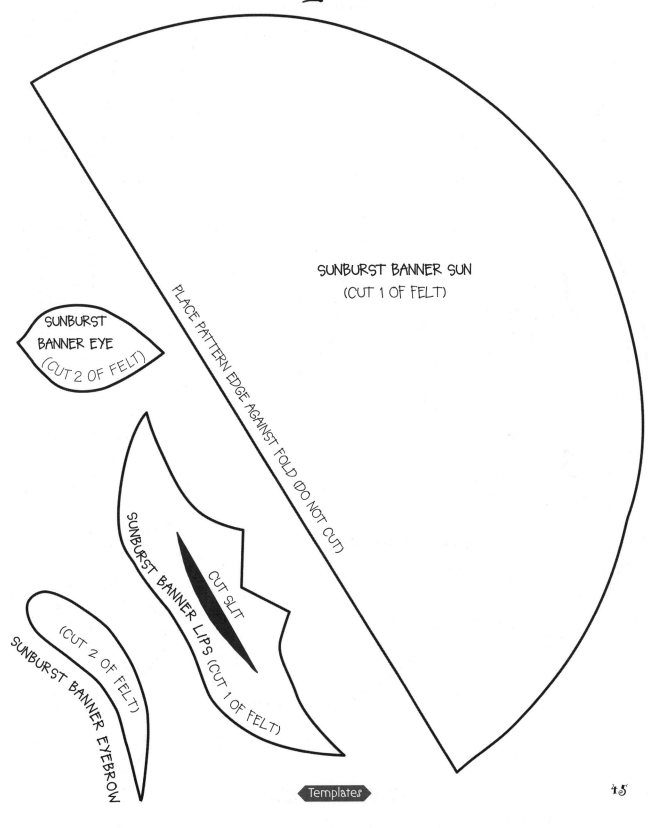

SUNBURST BANNER SUN
(CUT 1 OF FELT)

SUNBURST BANNER EYE
(CUT 2 OF FELT)

PLACE PATTERN EDGE AGAINST FOLD (DO NOT CUT)

SUNBURST BANNER LIPS (CUT 1 OF FELT)

CUT SLIT

(CUT 2 OF FELT)

SUNBURST BANNER EYEBROW

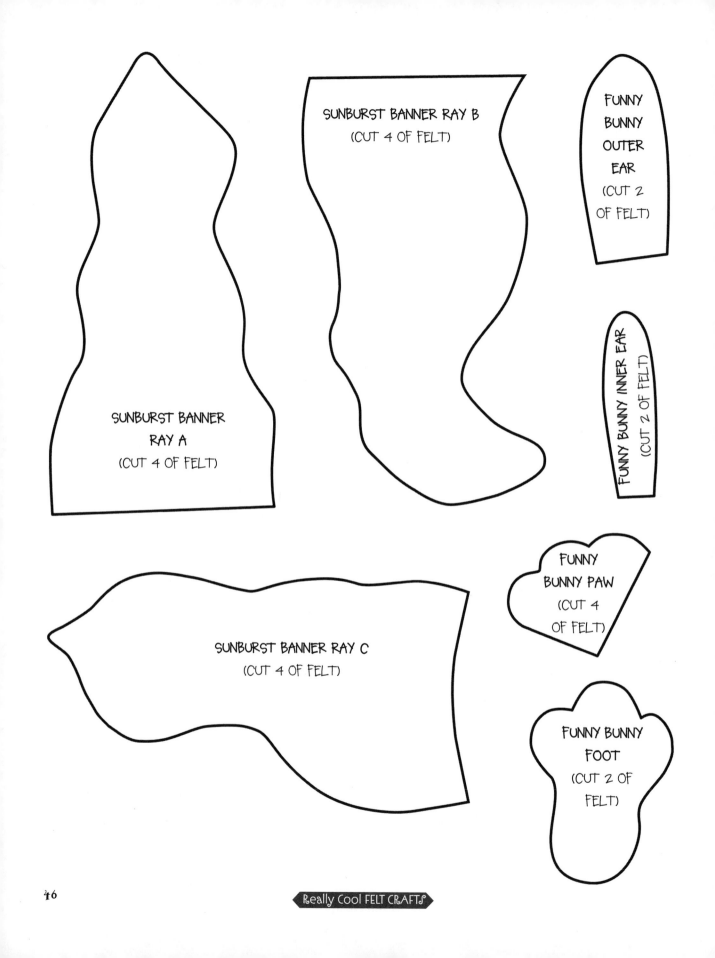

SUNBURST BANNER RAY B
(CUT 4 OF FELT)

FUNNY
BUNNY
OUTER
EAR
(CUT 2
OF FELT)

SUNBURST BANNER
RAY A
(CUT 4 OF FELT)

FUNNY BUNNY INNER EAR
(CUT 2 OF FELT)

FUNNY
BUNNY PAW
(CUT 4
OF FELT)

SUNBURST BANNER RAY C
(CUT 4 OF FELT)

FUNNY BUNNY
FOOT
(CUT 2 OF
FELT)

FUNNY
BUNNY
CARROT
(CUT 6
OF FELT)

FIDO BONE
(CUT 2 OF FELT)

FUNNY BUNNY BODY
(CUT 2 OF FELT)

FIDO DISH/BIRD NEST
(CUT 2 OF FELT FOR EACH)

BABY
BIRD TAIL
FEATHER
(CUT 1
OF FELT)

BABY BIRD
WING
(CUT 2 OF
FELT)

MOTHER BIRD WING
(CUT 2 OF FELT)

BABY BIRD BODY
(CUT 2 OF FELT)

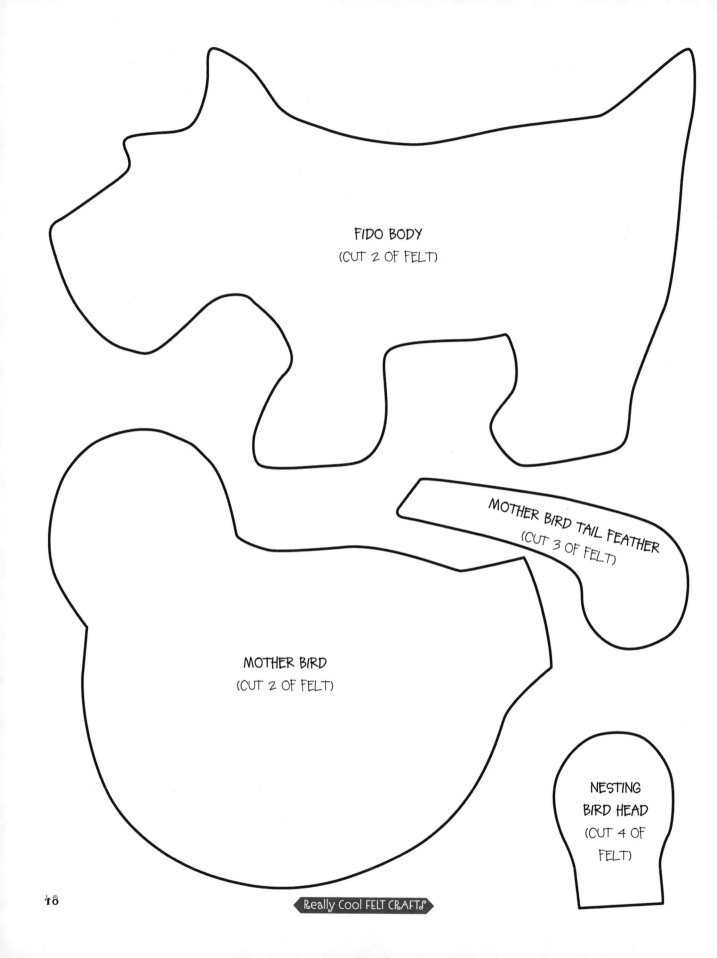

FIDO BODY
(CUT 2 OF FELT)

MOTHER BIRD TAIL FEATHER
(CUT 3 OF FELT)

MOTHER BIRD
(CUT 2 OF FELT)

NESTING
BIRD HEAD
(CUT 4 OF
FELT)

Really Cool FELT CRAFTS

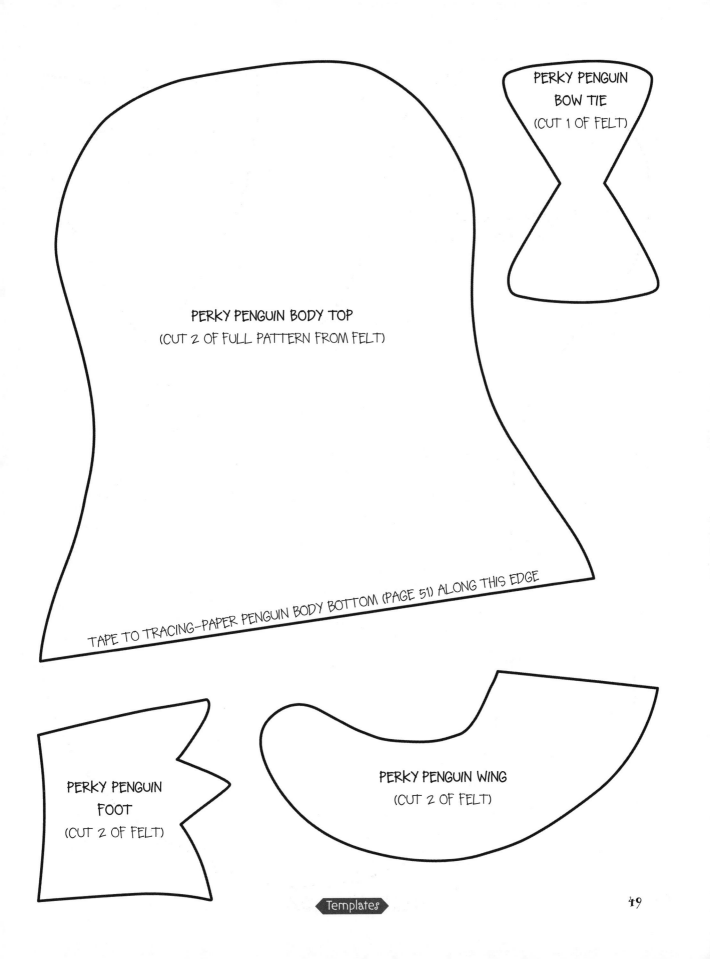

PERKY PENGUIN
BOW TIE
(CUT 1 OF FELT)

PERKY PENGUIN BODY TOP
(CUT 2 OF FULL PATTERN FROM FELT)

TAPE TO TRACING-PAPER PENGUIN BODY BOTTOM (PAGE 51) ALONG THIS EDGE

PERKY PENGUIN
FOOT
(CUT 2 OF FELT)

PERKY PENGUIN WING
(CUT 2 OF FELT)

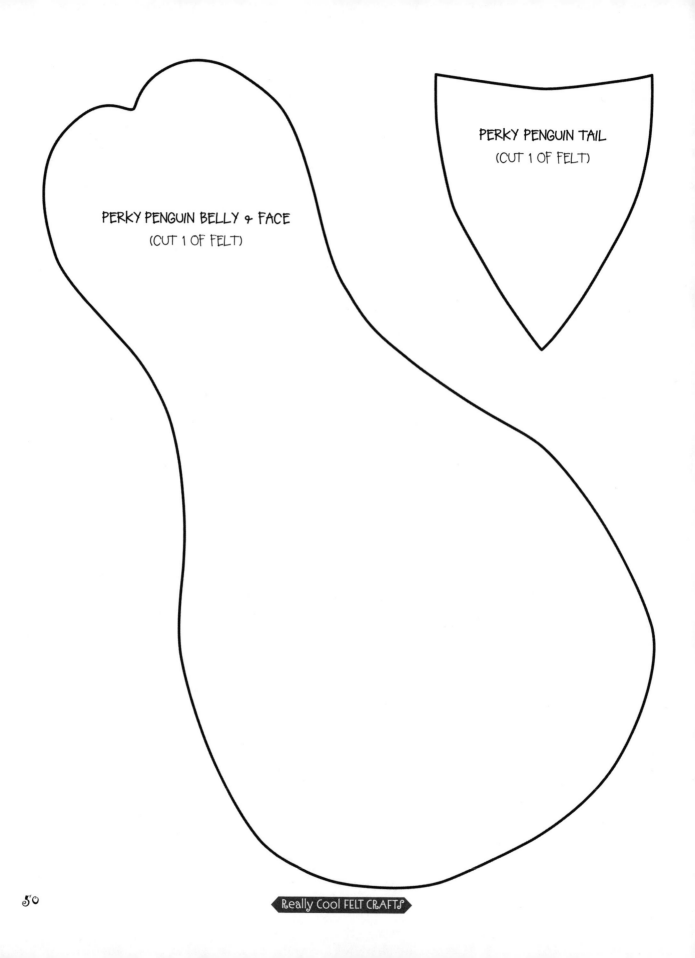

PERKY PENGUIN TAIL
(CUT 1 OF FELT)

PERKY PENGUIN BELLY & FACE
(CUT 1 OF FELT)

Really Cool FELT CRAFTS

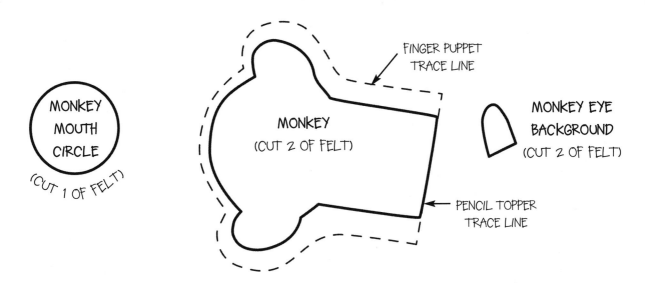

MONKEY
MOUTH
CIRCLE

(CUT 1 OF FELT)

FINGER PUPPET
TRACE LINE

MONKEY
(CUT 2 OF FELT)

MONKEY EYE
BACKGROUND
(CUT 2 OF FELT)

PENCIL TOPPER
TRACE LINE

TAPE TO TRACING-PAPER PENGUIN BODY TOP (PAGE 49) ALONG THIS EDGE

PERKY PENGUIN BODY BOTTOM
(CUT 2 OF FULL PATTERN FROM FELT)

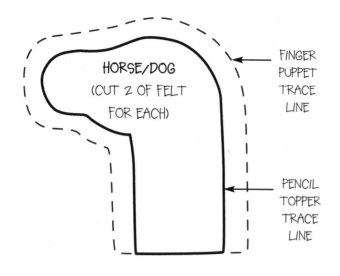

HORSE/DOG
(CUT 2 OF FELT
FOR EACH)

FINGER PUPPET TRACE LINE

PENCIL TOPPER TRACE LINE

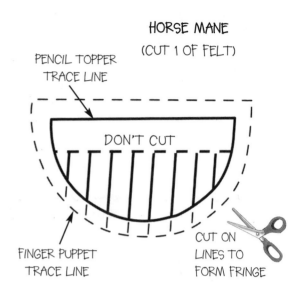

HORSE MANE
(CUT 1 OF FELT)

PENCIL TOPPER TRACE LINE

DON'T CUT

FINGER PUPPET TRACE LINE

CUT ON LINES TO FORM FRINGE

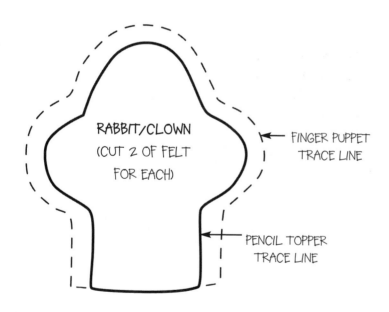

RABBIT/CLOWN
(CUT 2 OF FELT
FOR EACH)

FINGER PUPPET TRACE LINE

PENCIL TOPPER TRACE LINE

(see page 54 for the other three CLOWN templates)

RABBIT CHEEK
(CUT 2 OF FELT)

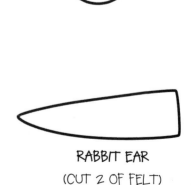

RABBIT EAR
(CUT 2 OF FELT)

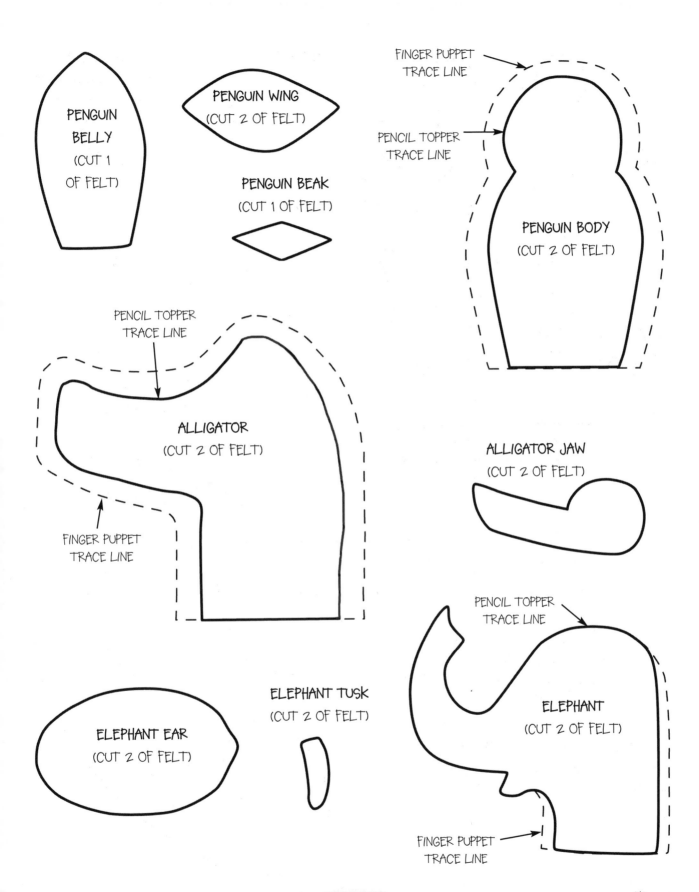

PENGUIN BELLY
(CUT 1 OF FELT)

PENGUIN WING
(CUT 2 OF FELT)

PENGUIN BEAK
(CUT 1 OF FELT)

FINGER PUPPET TRACE LINE

PENCIL TOPPER TRACE LINE

PENGUIN BODY
(CUT 2 OF FELT)

PENCIL TOPPER TRACE LINE

ALLIGATOR
(CUT 2 OF FELT)

FINGER PUPPET TRACE LINE

ALLIGATOR JAW
(CUT 2 OF FELT)

PENCIL TOPPER TRACE LINE

ELEPHANT
(CUT 2 OF FELT)

ELEPHANT TUSK
(CUT 2 OF FELT)

ELEPHANT EAR
(CUT 2 OF FELT)

FINGER PUPPET TRACE LINE

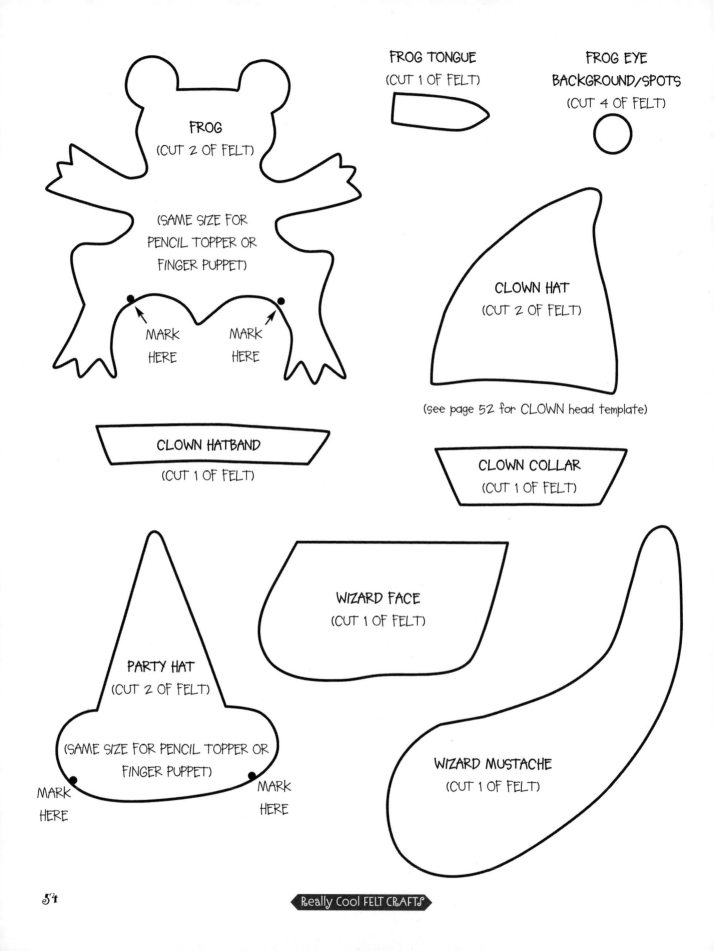

FROG TONGUE
(CUT 1 OF FELT)

FROG EYE
BACKGROUND/SPOTS
(CUT 4 OF FELT)

FROG
(CUT 2 OF FELT)

(SAME SIZE FOR
PENCIL TOPPER OR
FINGER PUPPET)

MARK
HERE

MARK
HERE

CLOWN HAT
(CUT 2 OF FELT)

(see page 52 for CLOWN head template)

CLOWN HATBAND
(CUT 1 OF FELT)

CLOWN COLLAR
(CUT 1 OF FELT)

WIZARD FACE
(CUT 1 OF FELT)

PARTY HAT
(CUT 2 OF FELT)

(SAME SIZE FOR PENCIL TOPPER OR
FINGER PUPPET)

MARK
HERE

MARK
HERE

WIZARD MUSTACHE
(CUT 1 OF FELT)

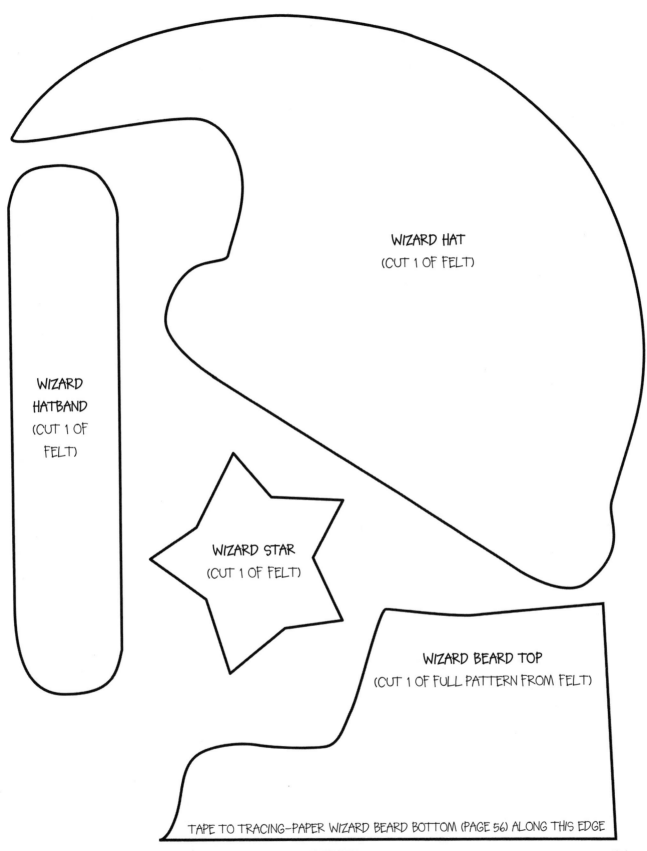

WIZARD HAT
(CUT 1 OF FELT)

WIZARD
HATBAND
(CUT 1 OF
FELT)

WIZARD STAR
(CUT 1 OF FELT)

WIZARD BEARD TOP
(CUT 1 OF FULL PATTERN FROM FELT)

TAPE TO TRACING-PAPER WIZARD BEARD BOTTOM (PAGE 56) ALONG THIS EDGE

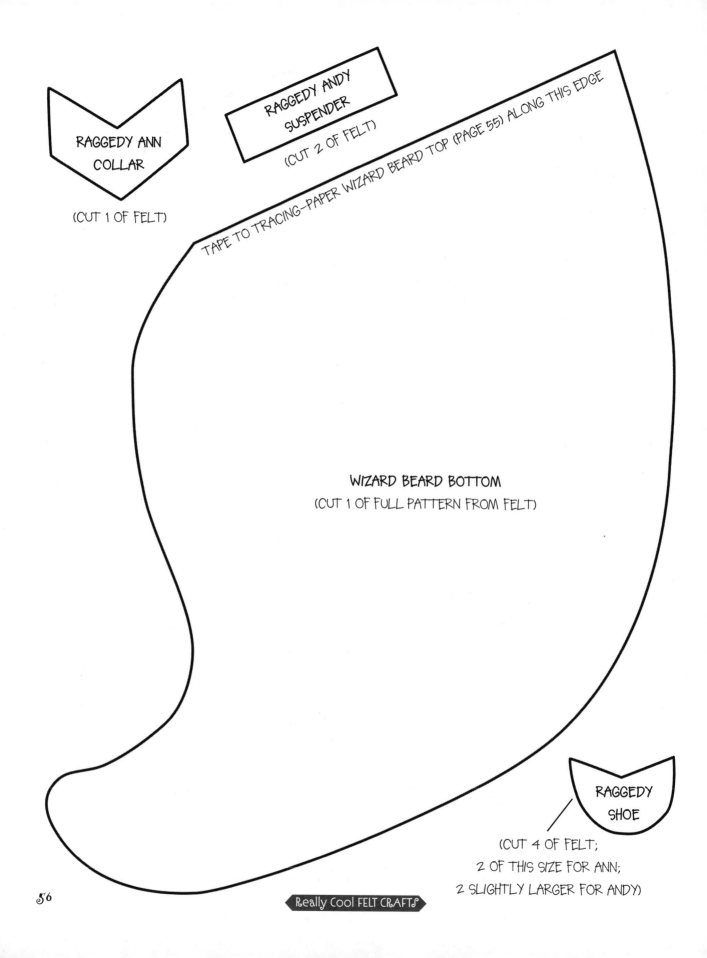

RAGGEDY ANN
COLLAR

(CUT 1 OF FELT)

RAGGEDY ANDY
SUSPENDER

(CUT 2 OF FELT)

TAPE TO TRACING-PAPER WIZARD BEARD TOP (PAGE 55) ALONG THIS EDGE

WIZARD BEARD BOTTOM
(CUT 1 OF FULL PATTERN FROM FELT)

RAGGEDY
SHOE

(CUT 4 OF FELT;
2 OF THIS SIZE FOR ANN;
2 SLIGHTLY LARGER FOR ANDY)

Really Cool FELT CRAFTS

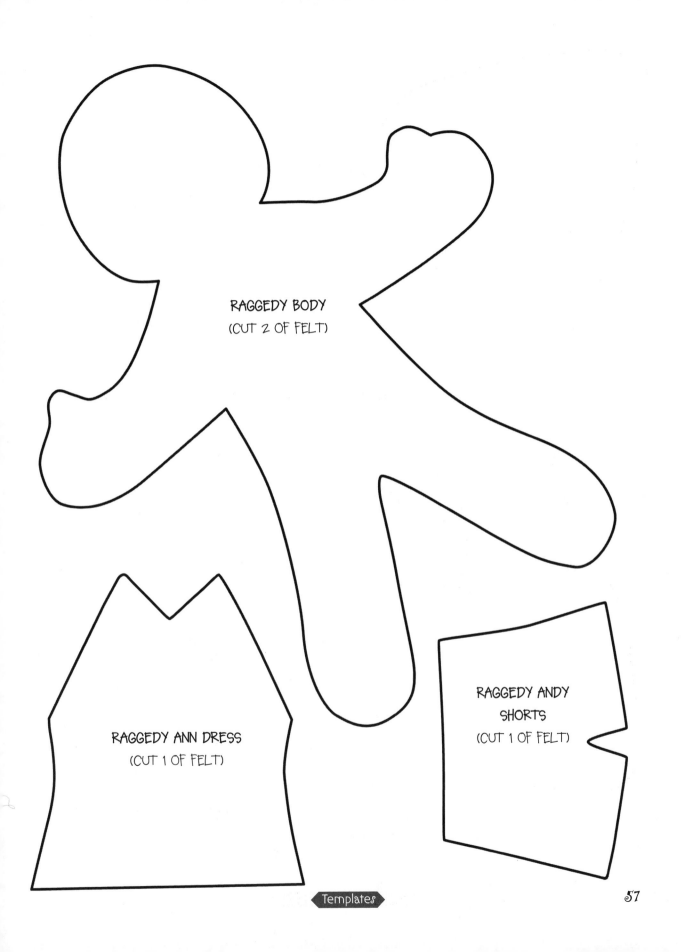

RAGGEDY BODY
(CUT 2 OF FELT)

RAGGEDY ANN DRESS
(CUT 1 OF FELT)

RAGGEDY ANDY
SHORTS
(CUT 1 OF FELT)

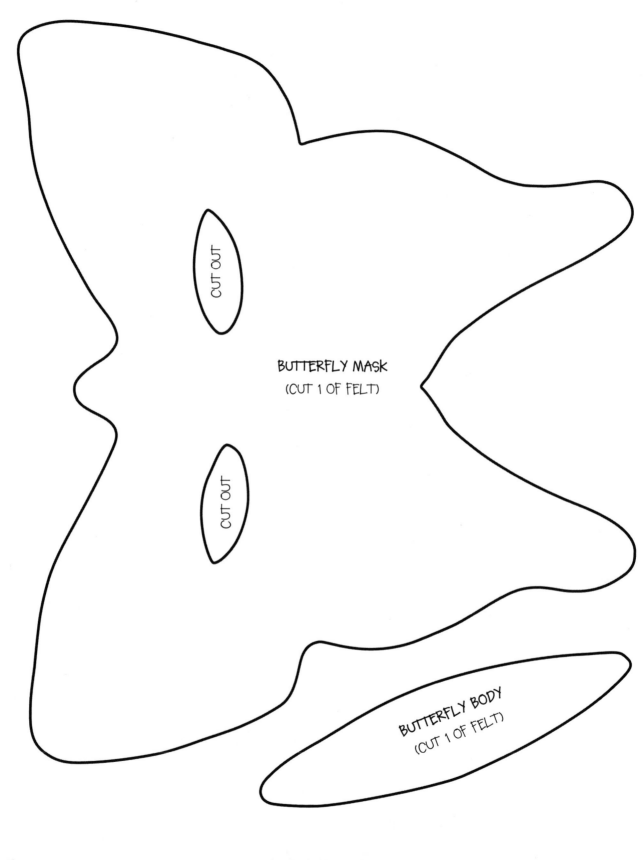

CUT OUT

CUT OUT

BUTTERFLY MASK
(CUT 1 OF FELT)

BUTTERFLY BODY
(CUT 1 OF FELT)

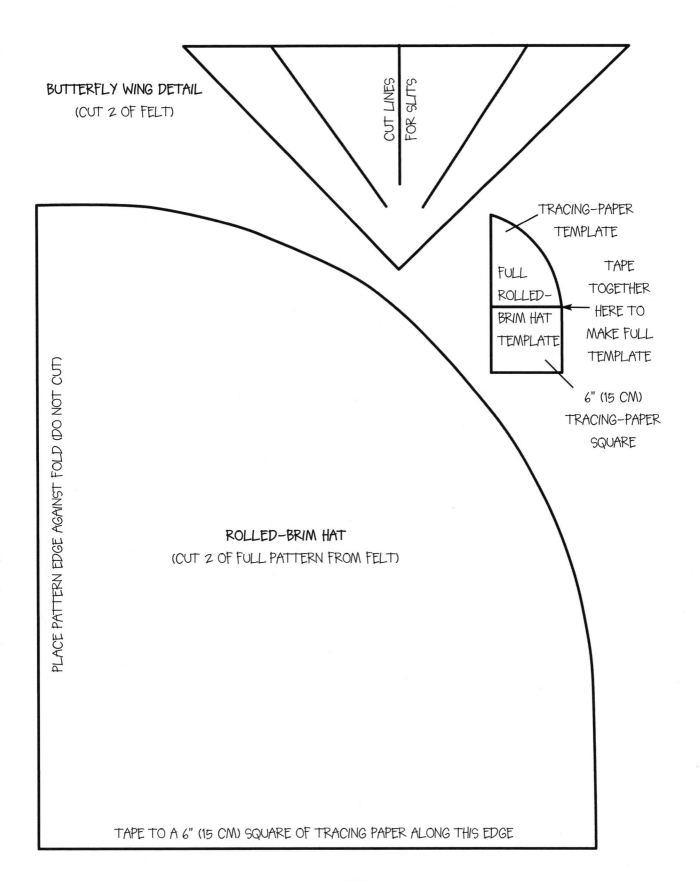

BUTTERFLY WING DETAIL
(CUT 2 OF FELT)

CUT LINES FOR SLITS

TRACING-PAPER TEMPLATE

FULL ROLLED-BRIM HAT TEMPLATE

TAPE TOGETHER HERE TO MAKE FULL TEMPLATE

6" (15 CM) TRACING-PAPER SQUARE

PLACE PATTERN EDGE AGAINST FOLD (DO NOT CUT)

ROLLED-BRIM HAT
(CUT 2 OF FULL PATTERN FROM FELT)

TAPE TO A 6" (15 CM) SQUARE OF TRACING PAPER ALONG THIS EDGE

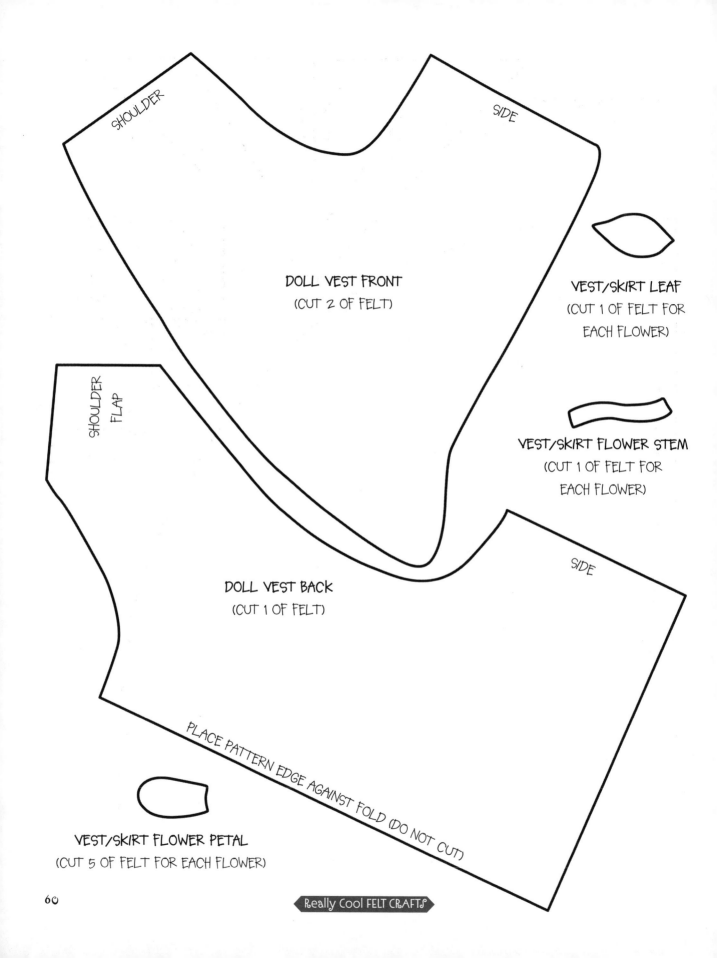

SHOULDER

SIDE

DOLL VEST FRONT
(CUT 2 OF FELT)

VEST/SKIRT LEAF
(CUT 1 OF FELT FOR
EACH FLOWER)

SHOULDER FLAP

VEST/SKIRT FLOWER STEM
(CUT 1 OF FELT FOR
EACH FLOWER)

DOLL VEST BACK
(CUT 1 OF FELT)

SIDE

PLACE PATTERN EDGE AGAINST FOLD (DO NOT CUT)

VEST/SKIRT FLOWER PETAL
(CUT 5 OF FELT FOR EACH FLOWER)

Really Cool FELT CRAFTS

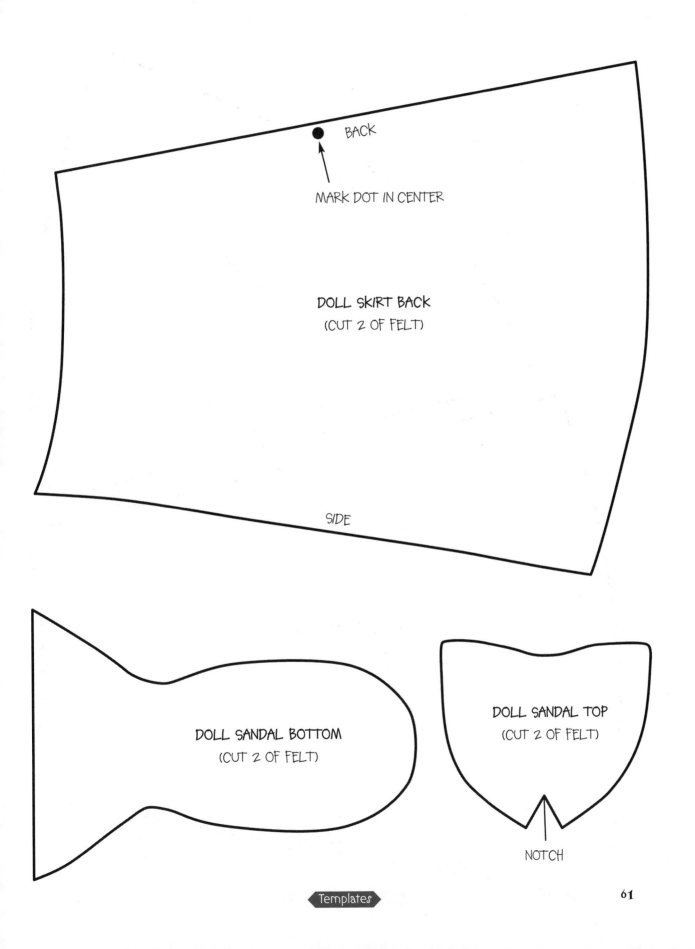

BACK

MARK DOT IN CENTER

DOLL SKIRT BACK
(CUT 2 OF FELT)

SIDE

DOLL SANDAL BOTTOM
(CUT 2 OF FELT)

DOLL SANDAL TOP
(CUT 2 OF FELT)

NOTCH

Templates

DOLL HAT

(CUT 2 OF FELT)

PLACE PATTERN EDGE AGAINST FOLD (DO NOT CUT)

SIDE

DOLL SKIRT FRONT

(CUT 1 OF FELT)

CENTER

PLACE PATTERN EDGE AGAINST FOLD (DO NOT CUT)

Really Cool FELT CRAFTS

Index

More Good Books from Williamson Publishing

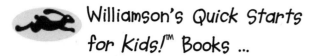

Williamson's Quick Starts for Kids!™ Books ...

Quick Starts for Kids!™ books, for children ages 8 and older, are each 64 pages, fully illustrated, trade paper, 8 x 10, $7.95 US/$10.95 CAN.

> **Also by Peg Blanchette & Terri Thibault!**
>
> KIDS' EASY KNITTING PROJECTS
> by Peg Blanchette
>
> KIDS' EASY QUILTING PROJECTS
> by Terri Thibault

DRAWING HORSES
(that look *real!*)
by Don Mayne

MAKE YOUR OWN CHRISTMAS ORNAMENTS
by Ginger Johnson

GARDEN FUN!
Indoors & Out; In Pots & Small Spots
by Vicky Congdon

40 KNOTS TO KNOW
Hitches, Loops, Bends & Bindings
by Emily Stetson

MAKE YOUR OWN FUN PICTURE FRAMES!
by Matt Phillips

MAKE YOUR OWN HAIRWEAR
Beaded Barrettes, Clips, Dangles & Headbands
by Diane Baker

Parents' Choice Approved
BAKE THE BEST-EVER COOKIES!
by Sarah A. Williamson

BE A CLOWN!
Techniques from a Real Clown
by Ron Burgess

Dr. Toy 100 Best Children's Products
Dr. Toy 10 Best Socially Responsible Products
MAKE YOUR OWN BIRDHOUSES & FEEDERS
by Robyn Haus

YO-YO!
Tips & Tricks from a Pro
by Ron Burgess

Oppenheim Toy Portfolio Gold Award
DRAW YOUR OWN CARTOONS!
by Don Mayne

American Bookseller Pick of the Lists
**MAKE YOUR OWN TEDDY BEARS
& BEAR CLOTHES**
by Sue Mahren

To Order Books:

Toll-free phone orders with credit cards:
1-800-234-8791

We accept Visa and MasterCard *(please include the number and expiration date).*

Fax orders with credit cards:
1-800-304-7224

Or, send a check with your order to:

**Williamson Publishing Company
P.O. Box 185
Charlotte, Vermont 05445**

Catalog request: mail, phone, or e-mail

info@williamsonbooks.com

Please add **$4.00** for postage for one book plus **$1.00** for each additional book. Satisfaction is guaranteed or full refund without questions or quibbles.

Visit Our Website!
www.williamsonbooks.com